Goodbye Stress

By

Anand Alagappan

Copyright © 2019 Anand Alagappan. All rights reserved

**ISBN:** 978-0-9857040-3-2

## Chapters

1. Introduction — 1
2. Mind — 3
3. Aspects of mind — 6
4. Mind investigation — 10
5. Body — 14
6. External world — 16
7. Consciousness — 25
8. Stress — 28

## Introduction

Stress is a much talked about word these days. You hear it everywhere from media to office, home, hospitals, colleges, social media etc. It's talked about to an extent that even if you don't have stress you will feel like you are missing out something and have second thoughts about it.

Life definitely wasn't easy when you grew up. But did your parents talk about stress this much as you do it today. Or was it always there and only because of communication and internet you are talking more about it today?

What is stress in the first place?

You have heard about worrying. Is worrying the same as stress? If someone who is constantly worrying, are they constantly stressed? Worry sounds more like a philosophical term associated with mind, whereas stress looks like a term borrowed from Physics meaning pressure exerted on a physical object.

You even have a point called a "breaking point", beyond which the object breaks if you apply excessive pressure. Something too much for the object to handle.

When you hear people say, "There's too much pressure at work" or "pressure at home", are they talking about a breaking point, a limit beyond which they are going to break down?

If you are lifting weights your body will tell you what is the limit. You can't run forever, can you? Common sense prevails and tells you "Stop, you have reached your limit". But then when you talk about pressure in office or home nobody is asking you to lift heavy weights which you can't handle. They are not asking you to do something physical beyond your limits. If that is the case the answer is a simple, "No, I can't. I know my limits".

You are today talking about stress at a mental level. So, stress indeed like worry is associated with mind.

Are you then saying stress is something too much for the mind to handle? What exactly do you mean?

To start with, do you even have a proper understanding of the mind before you talk about stress? Is it the inner voice talking to you constantly? Your thoughts or what is mind?

Too many question marks and what is the answer? Let's first get few definitions right so that you can find the right solutions.

# Mind

You have used the term mind colloquially many times in your life. Famous ones being, "Out of sight, out of mind," Are you out of your mind?", "Playing mind games", "The first thing that comes to my mind", "I lost my mind", "Sorry, my mind was somewhere else", "my mind processes things differently", "my mind is going crazy", "my mind said yes, heart said no", "mind is busy making plans", "I know exactly how my mind works", "I have a mind of my own", ""mind gets distracted", "It didn't register in my mind", "make up your mind fast", "back of my mind", "I can't read your mind", "change your mind", "What goes through your mind", "It's all in the mind", "open minded", "state of mind", mindset, mindless actions, mindfulness, mind boggling, mind chattering, monkey mind, control the mind, focus your mind, relax your mind, stretch your mind, clear your mind, racing mind, restless mind, logical mind, steady mind, brilliant mind, active mind, strong mind, fresh mind, sane mind, calm mind, peace of mind, quieting the mind, transcending your mind, beyond mind etc.

You don't realize how many times you use it without understanding it fully. So, what can you infer from the above phrases that so often you use?

It sounds as though mind is like a physical entity, like a thing, an object that has set boundaries doing something and that you can do something with, but is actually not. But it is present to the extent that you say, "I have a mind".

Let's look at some of the above phrases you use. Predominantly today mind is related to a thought or collection of thoughts. As human beings you have the ability to think and you call this faculty mind. You say things like - focus your mind, control your mind, quieting the mind, my mind gets distracted etc. These are all based on thoughts.

Thinking leads to thoughts. What then is a thought? Let's take a few examples to understand it.

**Example 1:**

Say you are reading news early in the morning. Suddenly you have a thought, "I have a meeting at 9 am. I better get going".

**Example 2:**

Sometimes you say your mind is busy making plans. You have seen this while lying on your bed, during meditation, listening to a lecture or when you are in a meeting. While the primary activity is something, your mind is busy doing something else. Your mind gets distracted and you then say focus your mind.

**Example 3:**

You forget your password. So, you start with, "Let me think".

Everyday your life is filled with all sorts of thoughts. Where do these thoughts come from? What exactly is happening? Where are they stored for you to be dispensed at a right time suddenly and retrieved at a later right time your convenience?

There's much more to mind than just thoughts, which you often relate to an inner voice, someone talking to you constantly. Your mind has more aspects to it.

## Aspects of mind

There are three immediate aspects of mind based on the phrases we saw earlier.

**Memory**

Your mind can replay your entire past from childhood like a movie. Does the mind have a memory then? If it does have a memory, where is it? You often say things like, "It didn't register in my mind", "It wasn't in my mind at all".

Take another example. You are writing an exam. The answers you get, are they stored and then dispatched to you or is it just spontaneous? When you say I forgot the answer are you saying you did not get a thought dispatched or was it not in your memory?

The mind does have a memory but it's just that you don't know where it is?

But doesn't matter where these thoughts come from, they drive your actions based on these thoughts. Sometimes good and sometimes bad that determines your experiences, which you call Life.

These experiences again have something more attached to it, the intelligence.

## Intellect

When you say, "My mind process things differently", "I know how my mind works", "brilliant mind", there's a certain intelligence, an intellect with a reasoning capability of the mind that assists you in understanding and analysing things and situations.

If something is red hot your mind tells you not to touch it. Many times with its reasoning capacity it tells you not to do things that are dangerous.

## Ego

The intelligence is sometimes dependent on another aspect called the "Ego". This forms the likes and dislikes, a personal identity. Sometimes you say, "I have a mind of my own". This ego protects this identity and sometimes brings disagreements, very difficult to let go, which you call stubbornness.

With all the above said your mind is pretty much like a helper or an assistant telling you things.

Say you wake up and you're still lying in your bed and your mind says, "Get up fast, time to go to office". It makes plans for the whole day while you are lying. Whether the day goes according to the plans or not is another issue.

But then is your entire actions and life driven by your mind? If you are walking you don't have a thought saying every second step 1, step 2, step 3. You just walk without thinking.

If you miss a street and you walk past you may suddenly realize, "Oh I forgot to turn left on that street" and you go back. So, the helper mind reminds you that you have missed it.

Not always these helping tips are good. Sometimes it can be bad. If someone is annoying the mind can say, "Punch him in the face." Or in spite of the warning that it's not good for your health your mind says, "It's okay take it". Are you going to take these instructions and execute it?

When you have to make decisions big or small you rely on your mind. Should I do it or not? Sometimes you say I just went with the gut feeling.

What you can infer from your own experience is that you cannot rely on your mind completely. This is the nature of the mind. You just cannot trust it fully. As much as it has helped you it has failed you many times as well.

When you cannot trust the mind how can you rely on understanding something like the truth and answers to other pertinent questions?

This brings to another question what drives all of action?

Let's take an example. When you are so engrossed in reading something with no distractions, at least for the time being you don't have any thoughts. Is the mind present at this instance? Or is there a single thought only that is assisting you in reading and you are not conscious about it? What drives this action of reading? Who is the doer when the mind is not present?

We say successful people had the urge to succeed. They were single minded in achieving their goals. Was their craving to succeed fed by a single-minded thought or were their actions driven by something else?

You have the craving senses on one hand and then you have a mind. In between there's you. Is it because of the senses craving, a certain urge you helper mind says, "It's okay feed the senses"? If the mind doesn't exist will the craving senses get what it wants?

The urge to do something like you want a coffee is it because of the senses or the thought?

Even though the body does the action they don't house all the thoughts? So, a very pertinent question for you to solve becomes where do thoughts come from? If it's not the body, then from where?

Your obvious step next is to look outside. The world you see through the eyes. Are thoughts coming somewhere from outside? Well, so far nobody has proved that the wind and the cool breeze is pushing all the thoughts into you from outside. Then from where?

When you have the least help the best way to investigate the thought is, through the thinking mind itself. Use its own medicine to find out its origin and whereabouts.

## Mind investigation

You start investigating your mind, a more detailed understanding of your mind and all things related to it. We saw earlier mind is not just thoughts but it has a memory, intellect and ego. The more you try and understand you realise it has more things associated with it as well.

Another very important aspect of the mind is, "Time". When you do the things that you like time moves very fast and when you do the things that you don't like even a few minutes feel like few hours and you say time moves slow. Time is very much a concept of mind.

What is moving fast and what is moving slow? Nothing is, actually. It's just the mind playing the trick.

Time brings another concept called "Duality". We will see about duality in detail in the next few chapters.

So, is everything the mind's doing?

When you have more questions and no answers this is when you say, "My mind is going crazy". What do you do now? Take a break, let go and come back. But whatever time you come back it's back to square one.

You understand that the nature of the mind is to create more and more thoughts, thoughts unlimited, which you call mind chattering. It's an ongoing, never ending process. Every full stop is turned into question marks.

Finding the source of your thoughts doesn't have a simple answer. You wish it was like a Blackbox of an airplane, like an organ itself from where all these thoughts originated and you can find it easily like other body parts. It simply isn't that simple. But reasoning tells you there has to be an answer to this challenge.

If you are someone who takes on challenges you are not going to let it go. Maybe you can say let me try something different here. Rather than the source let me try and understand what these thoughts are? The nature of these thoughts. That might give some insight.

Thoughts are nothing but wants and desires which needs an expression. Sometimes they find expression through your senses. How these thoughts impact the five senses through, which you experience life, that drives action?

You establish the fact that you have a body, you have a mind. You assign mind to the "invisible faculty". Meaning you don't see it through your eyes. It doesn't have set boundaries contrary to the body.

Now, let's take a few examples and analyse.

**Example 1:**

Say you have a thought that you want to smile at someone you know when you are walking on the street. Your lips go wide and you have an action called smile. It finds an expression, a good one.

**Example 2:**

Sometimes you think about the past may be childhood days or things that happened in the past. These thoughts come and go. The thoughts about past might be good or bad. Bad thoughts might affect you and needs an outlet for expression.

**Example 3:**

You have a thought that you want to have a coffee. Your senses start craving and you say, "I'm in the mood for a good coffee". You go and get a coffee. Your thought is fulfilled. In other words, your desire is fulfilled. Your senses are satisfied at least for now.

Say on the other hand rather than getting a coffee you resist. Well, let me not have it for whatever good reason. Your thought which needs an expression, a desire that needs to be fulfilled is left unfulfilled. This unfulfilled thought may trouble you for a while unless you let go of it or fulfil it.

There are powerful thoughts which pushes itself to find expressions. Some thoughts fade away with less or no impact. You say positive, negative, good and bad thoughts based on the experiences you go through. But whatever it is they are thoughts.

If thoughts don't trouble you what is wrong in having zillions of thoughts? Let them just come and go doesn't matter good or bad. But that's not the case. It guides you in making few decisions and that can be bad.

You have heard about thoughtless state. The famous Enlightenment. Is there really such a state as thoughtless state? Does the enlightened person just evaporate into thin air after enlightenment because they reached a thoughtless state? If you have no thoughts how can you even function, do action?

The answer is that there are moments in life where you do actions without the interference of thoughts. Flashes of moments happens without thoughts and then suddenly the thoughts come back again. Either because of an external situation or just like that.

More thoughts come back again because of the relationship you have with the external world which you call the universe. Sometimes called the material world. You experience this outside world through your senses. The 5 basic senses being sight, smell, touch, hearing and taste.

Let's understand the body that houses these senses and the material world it experiences in its entirety.

## Body

You analyse the body and how much ever intelligence it has, in the end it perishes. If you were given an assignment to put the most important secret, the answer, the truth somewhere safe would you put in a perishable body?

The body is subject to constant change and it's under the sway of time. Your body cannot solve your problems by itself. In fact, it's taking instructions from the mind. Apart from mind it's active and moving because of a something which you do not know what it is? In the end time wins and body loses.

Your body is an effect for a cause. It's an instrument to serve a cause. But you don't know what the cause is? Whatever the experience it goes through be it good or bad it doesn't make your body static, permanent.

Take any instrument for example, like an airplane, a car or a bicycle. It's there to serve in this case the cause of movement. You want to move a person or something from point A to point B. The instrument serves this purpose. Cause or purpose here is the movement and effect is the instrument which you call a vehicle.

If you take your phone for example the purpose it serves primarily is communication.

In the same way your body serves a cause which you are yet to find out, which you call "The purpose of life".

One of the reasons your body goes through pain and suffering is because of the limitations and incessant change. Change pushes limitations and when limits break there's pain.

Even though your body is perishable and subject to change it still serves an important cause a higher purpose. You need a healthy and strong body to serve this cause for the time it functions. That's why good food, exercise, asanas, which you call Hatha Yoga are all important to give it the strength and the energy it needs to fulfil the purpose it was created for. The body needs to be given its due respect.

Understanding the body is just one part of the puzzle and understanding the cause it serves, is another part. Sometimes the effect is so fascinating and magical you forget the cause.

Let's move on now to understanding the material world which the body experiences.

## Material world

You call what you see material world because you are able to perceive it through your senses. Day in and day out you wake up and you experience this material world. As the name suggests it's full of physical objects, activities, movements etc. A pertinent question anyone would ask is how was it created?

Let's try and understand with a story of the ancient times.

**Sage Narada and the Mango**

Sage Narada is known for his intellectual mischief. Wherever he goes he creates a problem mostly an intelligent one to be solved and this time is it's no different when he visits Lord Shiva and Goddess Parvati in Mount Kailash. As is customary to take something when you visit someone Sage Narada brings one mango and offers it to Lord Shiva. Shiva accepts it and when he is about to cut it Narada says, "Lord, the mango cannot be cut into two and should be eaten by only one person". Lord Shiva thinks, Well, Narada as usual is up to something and he gives the mango to Parvati. She also doesn't want to eat it since it cannot be shared with Shiva.

At this time their two sons Ganesha and Kartikeya enters the scene and finds out what is happening there. Each one of them wants to eat the mango. Parvati understanding the situation says, "We will have a competition and whoever wins the competition will get the mango". Sage Narada takes it upon himself to offer the competition as well. He says, "Whoever goes around the world three times and comes back first will get the mango".

On hearing this Kartikeya immediately takes his vehicle which is the peacock and starts to circle the world. Ganesha gets into the thinking mode and after much thinking he asks his parents to stand together and circles them three times. When they ask him what he was doing he says that his parents are his world and that they are the source of creation and circling them is equivalent to circling the world. Shiva and Parvati are satisfied with Ganesha's answer and gives him the mango.

Kartikeya comes back after a while only to see his brother Ganesha having the mango in his hand and learns what had happened.

Even though the popular interpretation of this story is Sage Narada wanted to find out which one of the two siblings is smarter this is a story for mankind as well. The important thing to note here is, "Can you go around or circle the universe?"

When you say go around, circle you are talking about an outside and an inside which is logically impossible to understand in a bigger context like the whole universe. Because of your limited senses what you see is what you get.

**Infinity**

You studied about Infinity when you were in school and college. You were taught, one divided by zero is infinity.

You have heard this term the "Infinite universe". In reality "Infinity" is a mystery to understand logically. Infinity means boundaryless, without beginning, without end. It looks very simple. But does it make any sense?

Say for example you have heard sky is an optical illusion and it's definitely not a dome. For understanding purpose even if you assume it's a dome, what is beyond that dome. If you say there's one more dome, then what's beyond that one more dome. So, this goes on and on and logically there cannot be an end. Because then, there is always the question, "What's after that?"

To put it simply, "Universe is not a box". There's no boundary or limit. It's limitless, infinite.

This brings you to the question what exactly is the world you see and how is it hanging in there? For something to exist even if it's long, at the end of it something has to hold it. When you say hold it, there needs to be a beginning and an end.

We have the sun, moon, earth and all the planets, the forces that keeps it in equilibrium and all physical objects we see and experience. How is it at all held together when there's no end and beginning? There's a vast empty space right in front of us on which the physical objects and planetary objects are moving around. Where does space itself begin and end?

If the space everywhere is continuous within and without then what is the relationship between you and the outside world.

This leads to a suggestion that the world you see may not have any apparent reality in the sense that it's not separate from you.

Again, the universe is not a box for you to say I'm different and the outside world is different and there's separateness. Logically the ultimate substratum whatever you call it, "Nothingness or Self or Consciousness or Brahman" has to be without beginning, without end and is just IS. You cannot break it, you cannot cut it, you cannot separate it.

You can't even say the universe is expanding. Because something has to be present first for something to expand. You say something is real when it exists, which means it has a set boundary. But the whole universe in its entirety cannot logically have a beginning or an end to have a boundary.

This infinity what brings impermanence to this universe and its physical objects. Everything you see is subject to change. If it were a box you can clamp it and can remain static. The grandeur, beauty, good, bad everything remains a projection without apparent reality because of infinity.

That's why the Upanishads defines something infinite as "*neti, neti*", "not this, not this". The moment you define, it becomes finite. If you set a boundary or a limit it becomes finite.

## Duality

So, the external world has to be a projection of the mind aided by time causing duality. Because of time there's space. Otherwise how can space by itself have a beginning and an end. Because of space there's a multiplicity of objects and phenomenon.

It doesn't matter whether you are sage or scientist or whoever you are, this fact that "there cannot be a beginning and end" is not going to change. It simply doesn't make any sense.

Nobody can say, "Wait a minute, I'll show you the end of the universe and prove it to you". Because every end has a beginning.

When you are subject to time, duality arises. When duality happens, separateness happens, it creates boundaries and everything becomes a play, which you call "Lila". Where there's a play there's a result.

Take the game of tennis for example. Player A and Player B plays. The game creates 3 possible results, either A wins or B wins or neither A nor B wins for whatever reason. You can find out the probability of the wins but you cannot guarantee the results.

Fixing duality is an oxymoron. If there's a winning formula and you teach both players that formula, can they both win? When you say Game on, there's result and you have to wait for the results. Time comes into play.

This is why you say, "Don't know what the future has in store for me". Even if the players decide not to play and sits on the couch you have a silent player called "Time" and eventually time wins, but you just don't know when.

Duality is an interesting concept, yet mysterious. The nervousness, anxiety, fear, worry is all because of duality. What is happening is, both or all players want the same thing, which is to win. For this to happen someone has to be made preferential and the others have to lose. Good times for you means bad time for somebody else and vice versa.

Not just for tennis, this is true of all actions what you call life. When you are alive you are made preferential over time. If you know who is going to win then there's no point in action at all.

Duality brings unpredictability. There's an old saying, "The best thing to do is, not start anything", which means anything you start will have a result, that may or may not go your way. So, you should be prepared for the consequences and shouldn't complain.

This is what it means when they say, "Be content". You have already started a few things and it has its own consequences and results. If you want to start more things then be strong and deal with it. That's how everything in life works.

If everything goes your way then being content doesn't make any sense. Even for a President or a Prime Minister of a country with all the powers at their disposal, things don't go their way as planned and they are subject to duality as well.

## God

Duality and the results we talked above brings another interesting concept called God.

It creates a room for someone who is the "Dispenser of results", whom you may call God or whatever name you like. In other words, if all that mind wishes come true then there's no God.

God then is not an invention of man, it's a consequence of duality itself. It's just there and you give it a name. Unfortunately, this dispenser doesn't get much credit during good times and success and comes to your mind only when the results are not in your favour.

Player A wants results in his favour as much as Player B. Same with everyone who is a fan of Player A and Player B. They all go and pray to God. Can God satisfy everyone?

If you know the result to all actions then people will say, "Stop dreaming", "Don't count the chickens before they are hatched." Even gods who came as avatars only told you how to live and they didn't change all the results to one's favour. Worst of all they came, they left.

One of the reasons God cannot come and say, "I'm the one responsible for everything" is because whatever mind perceives is under the sway of time and is impermanent. In that sense God also has to go through time if he's standing in front of you. That's why Gods look so human and it's hard to believe God, even if they come to earth.

No result is always in one's favour. This is the nature of duality. You may call it luck or god or whatever you want, based on which the results are granted. Whether it's your god or my god or everyone's god, they are all hopes that the results of all actions will be in your favour.

Be it health or any material thing, some results of your actions are in your favour and some aren't. But still for some people there's a belief and hope in what you call God, that it all will end well. This hope is what keeps them going.

**Mind projection**

Well, it's interesting news that the universe is without beginning, without end and may not have an apparent reality? How is it going to help you solve your problems?

Doesn't matter if you believe it or not it, whether it's a fact or not, at least it gives some insight about the external world that it cannot stand by itself without you, for there's no separateness because Infinity is not a box.

So, then maybe the external world is a projection of your mind? By fixing your mind you can experiment and see if it solves your problems.

Can mind solve its own problems? By now, you know fixing mind means more questions? Don't even want to go there again.

If mind is giving so much problems try and see what if mind is not there? What lies beyond mind? The only way is to find out for yourself. Because it's yours and not an entity that you can give it to someone else and have them check it out.

The mind itself needs to become a seeker. The best way is to transcend its own nature and see what lies beyond? For looking outside hasn't solved anything but only create more questions.

In a way you are reverse engineering everything. At what point you reverse engineer anything? You have something and you don't understand what it is or how it functions? You rip apart all available things and examine it.

We have seen earlier that mind has its own nature. Unreliable, always trying to look for logic in a logic less universe. Sometimes good, sometimes bad. That's what it is.

Only when it realizes that transcending its own nature and merging into consciousness that it can see the true nature of everything which is bliss, beyond time, beyond duality, eternal, unchanging, infinite. The mind then becomes a seeker of truth looking for right thing in the right place.

## Consciousness

The dharma of your true nature is pure consciousness. Dharma doesn't have a good English translation. But you can loosely say, "the very essence of", "the very nature of things", not something which you can change or cannot change.

For example, the very essence of what an elephant is, it is mighty and all its features that makes it an elephant. If this essence is not it's not an elephant. The very essence of tiger is, it is ferocious and all its features. Same way the mind has its dharma of what it is, it's very own nature. Duality has its own essence of what it is. The very essence of what a thing is.

Same way the very essence of who you are is, you are consciousness.

I'm consciousness or I'm Brahman ("Aham Brahmasmi", "I'm that") from a non-dualistic way is very different from saying, "I'm God" in a dualistic sense. Upanishads says "The knower of Brahman is Brahman itself". Because there's no separateness it's not like one meeting another and doing a handshake. It's union of the Self which you call "Yoga".

Truth can only be realized and it's not separate for you to define it and say this is what it is. Because words have its own limitations. When you are using language it becomes two, it becomes duality. This is why silence is more powerful than words. When they say in silence you find all answers it means you are transcending duality.

When there's two your unreliable friend mind comes into effect.

This is one of the reasons it's difficult for the mind to comprehend how the consciousness manifests into myriad forms as the external world which the mind is able to project. Only when it transcends its own nature can it truly understand that Brahman manifests as this universe and its myriad forms and yet it is unaffected by it and beyond it.

Transcending your mind do it as a standalone project. There's both good and bad which you call life. There should be an all-powerful, omnipotent source, whatever name you call it responsible for that. But that source hasn't directly come and told you "I'm responsible".

You can't fix all the problems of the world, for the problems are infinite as well. You then say, "Life is a journey not a destination".

The answer to the question, what is the reason for all the good things in life? is the same answer to the question, what is the reason for all the bad things in life? Because infinity is not a box, the universe is not a box, the external world is a projection of your mind, there's no separateness.

All the answers to the questions, the source of all problems and solutions lies within you. Whenever in doubt look at the sky, for infinity cannot exist by itself. That's why they say look inside you for all the answers.

Asking the right questions and getting the right answers makes all the difference. Upanishads says, "Know the one by knowing which all else is known".

So, the next step is to look for that one. Seek it until you find it. It is what you call Liberation, Moksha, Mukti or Nirvana meaning transcending duality. Beyond mind whatever is IS. Whatever name you call it, Self or Brahman or Nothingness or whatever.

Unless you find the source, your life is never complete.

## Stress

To understand stress, it's important to understand the mind, body, the external world and consciousness which we discussed earlier. To simply put it, since all actions have results because of duality your mind sets expectations and when this expectation doesn't match the results, that's when stress happens.

Your mind again becomes very active in the next act and it becomes never ending. And for a while if the results go your way, you say you are stress free. But when it doesn't, you say it's stressful.

Oftentimes you think it's the overwhelming amount of thoughts, which you cannot handle gives you stress. But from experience you can say, even a single thought, single action, if the results are not in your favour and gets delayed it adds to stress.

But at the same time, if the actions are overwhelming and the results are in your favour you don't feel very much stressed.

For example, if you are asked to travel the world, see new places, visit beaches nonstop, even if it's too much to handle, if all goes well you don't feel stressed. You push yourself, stretching your limits if your expectations are met. It becomes your liking.

On the other hand, say during that travel if things are not happening in your favour, as per your plan, it can be very stressful. You say I hate it. If you want to give it a formula

Stress is nothing but "Expectation **not equal to** Result".

$$\text{Expectation} \neq \text{Result}$$

Well, then how to get rid of stress? The answer is simple, let go of results and have no expectations. In a way, you are talking about letting go of duality itself, which again is transcending mind. But it's easier said than done.

It's easy to say let go of results unless you know the technique to do it. Three important techniques that helps you achieve this goal are - Bhakti, also known as prayer, devotion, Pranayama, the breathing technique and Dhyana, which today translates to meditation.

Bhakti is not just asking for things to go in your favour, give me this, give me that and give me more, but is simply a ritual to let go attachment to results. They say, "Do your duty and leave the rest to God". Krishna says in Bhagavad Gita, "You have the right to work, but not the fruits of the work". With the intent to surrender results indulge in bhakti in whatever form.

Pranayama, the breathing technique helps you be in the present moment and helps you surrender results.

Dhyana, meditation is to transcend the mind completely and realize a permanent state of consciousness, bliss.

As the Zen saying goes, "Before Enlightenment chop wood, carry water, After Enlightenment chop wood, carry water". You still do actions, but consciously where your mind and consciousness merges into one which you call Yoga.

The first two techniques are easier and helps you get closer to the goal while the third one with practise gets the job done fully.

About duality everyone said it differently. Buddha said there's Dukha, suffering. No matter who you are, what you are, all things in this universe are under the sway of time. When you say life is hard you are talking about duality, it's consequences and results. The only time life is easy is when all things happen your way.

The state of Yoga, transcending duality is an inexplicable state. You can say sugar is sweet but you have to taste it know it. In the same way have a taste of non-duality for what it is and realize it yourself. It needs practise as with anything else.

Practise is what makes everything perfect and this is no different. Practise it, even better make it a daily practise, call it "Sadhana".

Do your homework and be well!

31

www.ingramcontent.com/pod-product-compliance
Lightning Source LLC
LaVergne TN
LVHW040118080426
835507LV00041B/1725